ITIL4®:
The New Frontier

A Practical Guidebook for Adopting ITIL4®

Jeffrey Tefertiller
Service Management Leadership

ITIL4 ®– The New Frontier
Copyright © 2024 by Jeffrey Tefertiller
Service Management Leadership

Table of Contents

Service Management Leadership, LLC ▶▶

Foreword

Everyone has a unique story about how they were introduced to ITIL and when it really clicked for them that this framework would help them in their situation. Maybe you are new to ITIL and haven't had that "aha" moment yet. Maybe you are exploring the possibilities of ITIL improving your IT organization's way of work. Maybe you're further along your journey and have several certifications under your belt. Either way, the introduction of ITIL 4 is going to challenge what you know about IT Service Management and what it means to be a service provider that co-creates value with your consumers.

Jeffrey is no stranger to ITIL and has been a student of IT Service Management for years. Through his time at KPMG or being a trusted advisor to many businesses, Jeffrey brings experience and an understanding of best practice everywhere he goes. Whether through his podcasts, videos, or articles, Jeffrey's influence and leadership in the ITSM community is very apparent. Now you have the benefit of this experience as Jeffrey guides you through the transition from ITIL v3 to ITIL 4.

I was originally introduced to ITIL while I worked answering calls on the Service Desk at Orlando Health. Now serving as the Director of Service Management at AdventHealth I hold the ITIL 4 Managing Professional certificate. As I continue my learning, I have quickly gained a respect for the work Jeffrey does to help organizations capitalize on the benefits of IT Service Management.

My journey as a leader in the space of IT Service Management has presented many challenges that were previously not addressed by ITIL v3. This was frustrating as a leader and I found other IT leaders writing off ITIL because of the gaps that weren't addressed. ITIL 4 has since addressed some of these areas, such as DevOps, Agile, and Lean principles to incorporate best practice across the broad spectrum of information technology.

Whether or not your company is new on this journey of IT Service Management or your looking, like me, at how to incorporate the components of ITIL 4 that are shiny and new to your organization's current practices, this guidance will prove to be valuable. These talking points will give you the language and facts to help communicate to your C-suite and colleagues why this ITIL 4 journey is important and worth it. This guidance will give you the confidence to speak to what is new in ITIL and what areas you should focus on as you begin or continue your journey.

Kenny Hosey, ITIL 4 Managing Professional

Introduction

ITIL has led the maturity of Service Management for decades and should be lauded for driving progress in treating traditional IT organizations like a business. As one might imagine, the ITIL framework is delivering extreme value in some organizations while causing frustration in others, with most falling between the two extremes. We will examine the many reasons for success ... or lack thereof. One thought to keep in mind throughout is how every organization is unique, with a combination of variables that makes any specific company or government agency one-of-a-kind.

Since ITIL is a framework, it is meant to be applied in different ways, depending on the corporation's particular needs. It should never be considered a one-size-fits-all endeavor. There are far too many variables at play.

Achieving success relies on an assortment of factors. Think of the ITIL framework as analogous to making pottery. The potter, the wheel, the oven, the external environment, the mix and type of clay, the glaze, and even the time to cure determine the beauty and practical use of the product. Each potter puts his own individual stamp on his pottery.

If you have ever toured a pottery factory, you might have been amazed at how the people execute decades-old processes to create so many great outcomes. But these processes did not mature overnight. It took time to see what worked and what needed improvement. We only see the current state, not the journey to maturity. This is one reason comparison is for the foolhardy. Comparing one mature organization against an improving, yet immature, one will leave both sides lacking. The mature one will think they have everything solved and may stop improvement initiatives while the immature one may lose momentum or resources as the effort seems futile.

The same goes for ITIL within organizations. We see the current state, but we don't always see the external factors and process improvements that led to the current state. Just as the same pottery processes and external factors create different outcomes, it is true for the ITIL processes and framework as well.

Some believe in reviewing maturity and performance against industry benchmarks, but Service Management is one area where there are too many variables to give an accurate basis for comparison.

If we toured different pottery factories, we'd quickly perceive the outward similarity of their processes because the commonalities are readily apparent while the differences are subtle to the untrained eye. The differences in the finished pottery are the result of how the processes were put into practice.

With pottery, we are amazed at the beauty without considering all that went into the process. ITIL's impact on IT services should be similar.

Consider how the pottery and ITIL processes and practices are analogous. Think of the different kinds of clay as being like different types of changes or incidents, which vary among companies. Clay varies depending on the part of the world it is from and the type of pottery desired. The oven represents the production environment. Ovens look similar from the outside, but different potters use different kinds of ovens. The temperature and size of the oven will vary from potter to potter. Production environments are rarely the same. Every organization has basically the same environment from the view of external onlookers, but the unique architecture and the different software and hardware combinations will be organization specific. Each pottery company will have different procedures and timelines for curing its pottery.

8

In the same way, early production support, quality assurance, and criteria to hand over the new functionality to operations will depend on the company. The uniqueness of every organization will create its own IT services, just like with the pottery companies.

When previous ITIL versions came out, companies adopted the new framework over time. Similarly, every organization will make decisions about adopting this new version over the coming months and even years. This book will equip leaders to embrace and transition to ITIL4. The changes are significant, so the strategy must be thorough and the execution tight. The strategies in this book are adaptable for all organizations.

Some organizations have excellent Service Management programs while others face challenges. The reasons are many, but leadership support for Service Management and striking the balance of governance versus bureaucracy have been deciding factors of success for an increasing percentage of companies and government agencies.

With this in mind, a new ITIL version – ITIL4 – was recently published. This book will describe many of the strategies and opportunities associated with adopting and adapting ITIL4 and will provide guidance about how to do so.

We have done the research, talked to many experts, examined ITIL4, and compiled practical advice for implementing ITIL4. Through this process, we have developed a unique methodology that accommodates all industries, sizes, and types of organizations with differing states of maturity.

Whether you are happy with your current Service Management program – or not – we will provide you a path to adopting ITIL4. We will even address those who decide not to make the transition right now.

Some ITIL purists dislike the word "implement" when discussing incorporating the ITIL4 framework. They prefer the ITIL phrase of "adopt and adapt." If an organization is to adopt the framework, it must then be adapted to the organization. In an effort not to offend, we will use the word "implement" sparingly. However, "implement" is a common word in technology organizations and conveys a shared meaning understood by all.

In our research and conversations, the common refrain centers around how to be successful with ITIL4 if the previous versions were less than successful. Sure, the Service Management organizations that are thriving have many aspects in place for ITIL4 to be successful. But it is those who have one – or more - lacking Critical Success Factors (CSFs) that need the extra guidance.

10

There is an entire chapter dedicated to CSFs, KPIs, and metrics in general. Based on our research, the following table displays the percentage of time that a given reason caused ITILV3-based Service Management initiatives to fall short of expectations.

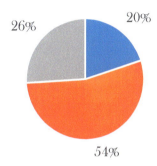

26%   20%

54%

- Leadership Support
- Initial Deployment or Ongoing Execution
- Lack of Customer Focus

Since there is rarely just **ONE** main reason or cause of unmet expectations, the percentages in the table below total greater than 100%.

11

%	REASON FOR UNMET EXPECTATIONS
39%	Lack of organizational and leadership support for both project resources and follow through. The best process will die on the vine without support.
36%	ITILV3 was originally poorly employed in organizations because organization leadership did not know how best to leverage the framework or used the wrong partner for the effort.
33%	Leadership belief that ITSM tool implementation would automatically result in process maturity. Maturity is independent of any and all tools; it is about standardization and repeatability.
33%	Lack of leadership's ability to convey Service Management value to colleagues.
32%	No Service Management Office (SMO) oversight or governance of the Service Management processes.
31%	Poor balance of governance to bureaucracy creating barriers to innovation and adoption.
29%	Low customer satisfaction (CSAT) with the Service Management processes (or CSAT not captured).
23%	Lack of stakeholder engagement which leads to lack of involvement, adoption, feedback, and funding.
22%	Shifting organizational priorities, resulting in resource deficit to continue maturing the Service Management organization.

%	REASON FOR UNMET EXPECTATIONS
21%	Lack of consistent process execution and delivery, leaving some changes – but not all - going through the Change Management group. Same for Incident Management, Request Fulfillment, and the other processes.
20%	Increased leadership turnover creating ever-changing goals and objectives. This is a huge issue for many organizations.
19%	Too much focus on the ITSM toolset to solve all the problems when it takes a balanced view of people, process, and tools to have process maturity.
18%	Habit of being in reactive mode (firefighting) so the SMEs and leaders are unable to get high enough to see the bigger picture. One cannot improve while mired in reactive mode.
18%	Lack of investment in process assessments to get an objective view of the Service Management landscape.
18%	Too many processes or too much change was attempted at one time. The organizational culture cannot handle the rate of change.
18%	Lack of quality metrics and measures – including KPIs and CSFs – to measure progress and identify improvement opportunities. This would have been higher, but the ITSM toolsets have metrics built in.

%	REASON FOR UNMET EXPECTATIONS
18%	Lack of focus on improvement. When we stop improving, we begin to atrophy, and momentum is lost.
17%	The Configuration Management Database (CMDB) had too much initial scope, making its success impossible. The CMDB is the foundation of all Service Management processes. It must be strong and stable to support a maturing Service Management organization.
16%	An increase in technology outside of traditional IT, leaving IT-centric processes in a difficult position if not mature enough to grow. This scenario should be seen as an opportunity, not a threat.
14%	Lack of a common lexicon for the organization to gain adoption. For example, there is no way you will mature the Incident Management process if an "incident" is called by several names. The same goes for a request, change, event, or asset.
14%	Lack of Service Management personnel development. These are difficult jobs. There is no school to attend to be a change manager or major incident manager, so these roles are best filled internally, and personnel need to be groomed for the future.

%	REASON FOR UNMET EXPECTATIONS
14%	Lack of Service Management process training, resulting in poor execution and lack of stakeholder adoption.
14%	Lack of a "front door" resulting in multiple Incident Management, Request Fulfillment, and Change Management processes.
14%	Service Operations was outsourced multiple ways where the focus is on meeting Service Level Agreements (SLAs), not process maturity.
14%	New technologies (cloud, Agile, DevOps, etc.) made Service Management more complex, and the organization could not congeal the "competing" frameworks.
12%	Low process maturity as a result of too many items on this Improvement Register. If the processes are not maturing, the support will wane, and other initiatives will override, even if they are less able to meet stakeholder objectives.

Wow, that is a big list, but still not exhaustive. We only recorded those with at least a 12% impact on the negative outcomes. The reasons are endless as to why some organizations could not take full advantage of the ITILV3 framework. Each of these items has some nuance that differs from company to company.

Many organizations were able to experience success with previous ITIL versions because the ITIL books – especially ITILV3 - went into great detail about each process, including process activities and metrics. The ITIL4 books are not as granular. We will unpack this more later in the book but understand that – as a rule – people like a step-by-step instruction guide and feel lost if there is ambiguity. Let's face it: we like having processes and procedures to follow.

While the ITIL framework may have achieved maturity to some degree in your corporation over the years, it was dependent on the individuals and uniqueness of the company. Think of the distinctiveness of your organization from the strategy (and strategic alignment) all the way through middle management and to the executive level. The human factor is represented many times. For others, the lack of process maturity placed a ceiling on the impact to the organization in creating an efficient and effective IT department. This book will discuss the newest ITIL version, ITIL4, and how it differs from the previous versions.

The most recent ITILV3 update came out over a decade ago and was implemented far more widely than previous versions. Its popularity can be attributed in part to companies' increased reliance on service providers, their need for increased governance and control, and their desire to quantify and understand costs while standardizing IT outcomes. There were other reasons as well, but these were the main ones.

In Chapter One, we will delve into more detail about ITILV3. It set the standard for how IT departments would treat technology like a business.

ITIL4 was published during the 2019 COVID-19 pandemic so organizations have been slow to adopt. The early adopters have experienced difficulty because, as mentioned above, it is much less prescriptive than ITILV3. Given that ITILV3 was prescriptive and still left many organizations desiring greater maturity, imagine how much difficulty organizations will experience with the less-than-prescriptive ITIL4. Incalculable. This practical guide should help you understand ITIL4 and how to transition it into any organization, no matter the maturity level of the Service Management program.

There are four things that are unique to every organization that will impact how ITIL4 should be implemented:

1. The risk tolerance of executive leadership.
2. The complexity of the organization.
3. The extent to which external service providers are utilized.
4. The speed with which leadership desires to adopt ITIL4.

Building on the last point above, adopting ITIL4 is a form of digital transformation, and it should be seen as such. This type of transformation can be used to support other transformations.

Why is it important to adopt the ITIL4 framework in every – OK, almost every – organization? There are two drivers for implementing ITIL4: a) the increased sprawl of technology outside of traditional IT and b) the increased usage of external service providers and cloud infrastructure. These two aspects are creating complexity in every organization, and the complexity is increasing exponentially.

18

Adding to the complexity is the desire for transformation. ITIL4 includes many aspects needed for accelerating transformation that were not within the purview of earlier versions. Consider the impact of Agile, Automation, Artificial Intelligence, Machine Learning, Blockchain, DevOps and Continuous Deployment, non-traditional technology in every part of the organization, and every other driver pushing innovation. Many ask whether ITIL4 and these frameworks (and their respective technology) are compatible. The answer is an overwhelming **YES!**

If you want high velocity, you must have guardrails and a safety net. For digital transformation at high velocity, the guardrail is ITIL4, and the safety net is a mature Service Management organization. Consider how everything that goes extremely fast (e.g., a rocket ship, airplane, etc.) has high quality standards to ensure that every aspect meets a high level of quality, including parts, architecture, testing, and even after-action reviews and documentation. These are the guardrails for high-velocity travel.

One thing to remember as you undertake this path: high speed and velocity require the ability to constantly reevaluate the controls and objectives, altering course as needed. This is the future of transformation. The outcome of the transformation will not be the stated goal at the start. Having a solid Service Management organization (via ITIL4) will enable the ability to take an incremental view of execution.

These are many of the reasons Service Management Leadership was formed and continues to provide value. Very few partners understand the Service Management world well enough to cater solutions to your specific organization, and its needs.

Chapter One – What is ITIL?
(And How Did We Get Here?)

Before we can discuss the newest version, we must examine how we got here. What is ITIL and why should we care? ITIL was first developed in the late 1980s by the Central Computing and Telecommunications Agency (CCTA), a Great Britain government agency. The lack of IT service quality procured by the British Government was the primary driver for the new framework. A method was needed to improve quality while lowering cost. For those not around at that time, technology was **VERY** expensive so understanding cost was a huge step forward. The CCTA soon developed recommendations for the effective and efficient provision of IT services. Interestingly, "effective" and "efficient" are two measures of IT services decades later. Effectiveness means to do the right thing. Efficiency is to do the thing right. The work resulted in a catalogue of best practices for IT organizations, which later became known as "ITIL." The earliest version of what we think of as ITIL was originally called GITIM, Government Information Technology Infrastructure Management.

Looking back, it would be difficult for a framework that sounds like "Get 'em" to gain widespread adoption, so it is no wonder that the name changed to ITIL. In a world of differing opinions, seeking best practice is the only way to standardize and improve the delivery of IT services. Back then, technology was centralized in the IT departments so improving service delivery was a primary goal.

Historically, IT groups were focused on software, hardware, and other technology, rather than customer requirements or even satisfaction. ITIL was developed with the customer in mind. One aspect every customer wants is standardized outcomes. The development and deployment of proven processes and clearly-defined responsibilities helped IT departments deliver better service at lower costs that still met customer requirements.

CCTA research found that the requirements of the various businesses and organizations were mostly similar, independent of their size or industry sector. Technology hardware is similar across industry and organization. So is software. ITIL has excelled with its universality. It is a framework to be adopted and adapted by any organization.

ITILV2 was released in 2001, putting guidance around lessons learned by the initial version. Reflecting back on the nature of how iterations work of all varieties, we know that the first version is adopted by many, then they put their flavor on things, minimizing the standardization of the framework. Then, the revision comes along and normalizes how the initial version was used and compiles the lessons learned into an updated best practice. ITILV2 was consolidated into nine publications. As you might guess, some of the publications were adopted more widely than others. The two publications most circulated and used were service support and service delivery, as organizations sought to improve the uptime and quality of IT services. These publications supported the very first use of external service providers.

In 2000, The CCTA merged into the OGC, Office for Government Commerce. ITIL was gaining in popularity as organizations were leveraging the power of technology at a growing rate. That same year, Microsoft used ITIL as the basis for developing their proprietary Microsoft Operations Framework (MOF). Microsoft understood the need for standardized service delivery. It was in the early 2000s that ITIL became the preeminent Service Management framework. Axelos now owns the publications and their rights.

23

In 2007, ITILV3 was published. It was a game changer for the way organizations thought about delivering IT services. Two areas that propelled ITILV3 to prominence: a) a focus on the customer and how they determined the value of an IT service and b) the introduction of the Service Lifecycle. The Service Lifecycle – still widely used by most organizations – included five phases:

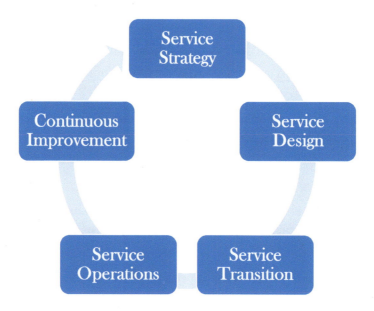

ITILV3 was so popular that many IT organizations were designed around the framework, with Service Transition and Service Operation getting the most attention.

After the fall of Enron, Service Transition became a focal point. Every publicly-traded US company had to have a viable Change Management process to document changes, segregate duties on testing approvals, and ensure the appropriate party's authorization. These requirements are referred to as SOX, or Sarbanes-Oxley. As the IT outsourcing movement grew in the mid-2000s, Service Operations was needed to ensure a standardized method for both internal and external service providers to deliver the services under their respective control.

In 2011, ITILV3 was updated to better focus on customer outcomes. A few new processes (e.g., Demand Management and Business Relationship Management) were customer focused while others (e.g., Service Level Management, Service Portfolio Management, and the warranty processes of Capacity, Availability, Continuity, and Security) were dedicated to improving the quality of IT services.

Given all the changes in technology, including innovation like the cloud, an updated version was needed. The increased usage of technology across every enterprise and new frameworks like Agile and DevOps necessitated the creation and adoption of the new ITIL version.

Chapter Two – What Changed in ITIL4?

The increased dependence on technology dictates a standardized method of service delivery. As technology moves outside of traditional IT at an astounding pace, Service Management becomes Enterprise Service Management. ITIL4 enables this shift as ITILV3 was not designed for the current role of enterprise-wide technology. Much has changed since 2007. The framework needed to reflect the changes.

In ITIL4, the traditional "Four Ps" of People, Products, Processes, and Partners become the "Four Dimensions of Service Management": Organizations and people, Value streams and processes, Information and technology, and Partner and suppliers. While it may not look like much has changed on the surface, notice the shift toward organizational change, attention to value streams, and different types of service providers. The rest of ITIL4 will illustrate this alignment with many common challenges in most organizations.

Another change in ITIL4 is the move from processes to practices. It may seem like semantics, but the ITIL4 authors wanted to change the perspective from repeatable processes to striving for excellence as in a practice (analogous to medical or legal practice).

Some practices were added, and others changed. Also, functions like the Service Desk became practices. The 26 ITILV3 processes became 34 ITIL4 practices. These are broken down into General Management, Service Management, and Technical Management practices. See the table below for the breakdown of each:

General Mgmt.	Service Mgmt.	Technical Mgmt.
1. Architecture Management	1. Availability Management	1. Deployment Management
2. Continual Improvement	2. Business Analysis	2. Infrastructure and Platform Management
3. Information Security Management	3. Capacity and Performance Management	3. Software Development and Management
4. Knowledge Management	4. Change Enablement	
5. Measurement and Reporting	5. Incident Management	
6. Organizational Change Management	6. IT Asset Management	
7. Portfolio Management	7. Monitoring and Event Management	
8. Project Management	8. Problem Management	
9. Relationship Management	9. Release Management	
10. Risk Management	10. Service Catalogue Management	

General Mgmt.	Service Mgmt.	Technical Mgmt.
11. Service Financial Management 12. Strategy Management 13. Supplier Management 14. Workforce and Talent Management	11. Service Configuration Management 12. Service Continuity Management 13. Service Design 14. Service Desk 15. Service Level Management 16. Service Request Management 17. Service Validation and Testing	

There are four main takeaways from the long list of practices:

1. The General Management practices are established to address the technology across the enterprise, not just in IT.
2. The Service Management practices are the traditional "processes" of old and seek to establish a mechanism to ensure the highest quality of services for the customer.

3. The Technical Management practices address much of the new innovations like DevOps and CI/CD, Automation, Machine Learning, and deployment methods, as well as others.

4. The one practice that gets the most discussion is Change Enablement. The ITIL4 authors sought to avoid the long-held homonym confusion of Change Management by renaming the traditional Change Management "Change Enablement" and adding the Organizational Change Management practice. Organizational Change Management is now a General Management practice in the table above. This name change will drive a couple of the "Potential Obstacles" in Chapter 6 as it will take time to change the terminology in all stakeholders' lexicons.

Two other changes in ITIL4 will be addressed in the next two chapters: the replacement of the Service Lifecycle with the Service Value System and the strategic use of Guiding Principles. To be successful in your ITIL4 transformation, you will need to understand these two key pieces of the framework. In this context, we must also mention two more areas we will go into greater detail about below: Governance and Improvement. Each depends on culture for success. The latter shows up everywhere in ITIL4.

Chapter Three – Service Value System

The Service Value System (SVS) is the centerpiece of ITIL4. Thankfully, while detailed and thought-provoking, it is not difficult to understand.

So, what is the Service Value System? The Service Value System is the new design structure for ITIL4. Think of it as an architectural diagram of the core elements and capabilities needed for a highly efficient, effective, and nimble Service Management program. It offers a high-level, end-to-end view of services consumed by business stakeholders. The SVS offers a view of how Opportunities and Customer Demand are turned into value. The SVS shows how ITIL evolves from a comprehensive set of processes to an operational model used to create value on demand. This is just one of many ways ITIL4 is less prescriptive than the previous versions. The components of the Service Value System are there to help you create value now and in the future. The components are:

- The 7 Guiding Principles
- Governance
- The Service Value Chain
- Practices
- Continual Improvement

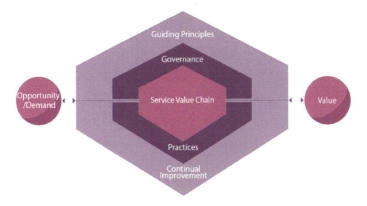

Prolonged success requires a repeatable mechanism – a system. When you have a solid system in place, your organization can achieve higher quality services at lower costs because all stakeholders understand the bigger picture.

The specific goals of your Service Management organization will mature over time. A growing and maturing SVS will help you to achieve these goals and objectives routinely. The SVS has built-in flexibility for organizations to grow and pivot course, as needed. Success is attainable through the design.

31

Service Management Leadership, LLC

If we think of the SVS from a "process" standpoint, it needs triggers, inputs, and process activities to create outputs. The inputs of the Service Value System are the Opportunities and Demands. These trigger activities within the system to create the output (Value). If Value is the goal, it is essential to understand what is being demanded and who is the customer making the request. Imagine a brick-and-mortar store not knowing what their customers wanted or even who their customer was. As ridiculous as that sounds, this was the IT model for decades. No wonder business stakeholders were frustrated.

When customers know what they want, it is a Demand. The keys are that the Demand must be understood by all parties and specific. There are several types of Demand, but we will just look at a few:

- Value Demand - The customer requires something specific, a product or a service. Usually, it is available through a service catalog and ordered through a self-service portal on the ITSM toolset.
- Information Demand - The customer needs to know something. The reasons can vary, but usually include the ability to aid decision-making. Some repeatable information demands are handled via a self-service portal or Knowledge Management system. The latter can be originated from a new or changed Product or Service (e.g., Known Errors after a new application goes live).

- Compliance Demand – The customer needs outcomes (Value) to meet compliance requirements. This type of Demand is increasing in importance as the regulatory and compliance requirements are rising.
- Failure Demand – The Demand arises from a Product or Service failure. Something happened and it now must be fixed, creating Demand. This scenario is played out every day in Incident Management. The Demand is usually captured through either the Service Desk (front door) or through direct input into the ITSM toolset.

Conversations with business stakeholders present opportunities to create new products or services, change how services are created and delivered, or identify an improvement. Consider how many types of new functionality business stakeholders request every year. Opportunities create new funding streams and offer the customer a new level of experience, a new capability, or a way to lower the cost of the service.

The difference between a Demand and an Opportunity is that the Demand is for something known and already available in some capacity, while an Opportunity requires innovation or a different way of doing things. Demands utilize current capabilities of the service organization, while Opportunities require effort to create new capabilities.

33

An Opportunity may trigger a project, require business analysis or stakeholder engagement, and necessitate an Organizational Change Management Plan. In short, Demands may be thought of as ordering off an established menu, while Opportunities require a new or changed capability and all that it entails.

The SVS supports both Opportunities and Demands and the goal for each is Value delivered to the customer, whether originating internally or externally.

Chapter Eight goes into more detail regarding Critical Success Factors (CSFs) and Key Performance Indicators (KPIs). As we will see, it is important to note their respective roles in measuring interactions with the business stakeholders. The most important metrics and measurements are those that measure what is important to our customers. Rising to the top of the list are the following with an example of each:

- Demands – How quickly are we fulfilling these requests?
- Opportunities – Are the requests for new functionality met with embrace or pushback? Further, a measurement may include the impact on legacy systems and resources compared to what the customers desire and require.

- Value (output) – Is the finished product on time, on budget, and are there metrics and measures to quantify performance and compliance?

We should ALWAYS be measuring the quality of the service delivered to business stakeholders. Always.

We discuss the Guiding Principles in the next chapter, so we will not get into much detail here. But consider the seven ITIL4 Guiding Principles as the lens leaders use to set direction. They are broad and general in nature, leaving the interpretation and execution up to the leader. We will leverage these Guiding Principles in our implementation strategies and execution.

Governance has become a profane word to some but is needed now more than ever. To some, it is unneeded "red tape". ITIL4 defines Governance as the means by which an organization is directed and controlled. If organizations want to accelerate change, they need Governance as the guardrails that permit speed and velocity.

Governance is a broad topic that can be implemented or defined in many unique ways. Much will depend on what needs to be governed and the organizational culture. Striking the balance of Governance versus Bureaucracy is difficult for many organizations. Guardrails are needed for all organizations and initiatives, but how much is too much? It depends on the organization. Governance usually comes from the top: The Board of Directors and includes minimizing the risk that concerns the Board. It starts with policymaking and a level of enforcement the culture will accept. The next level of Governance lies at the executive level to protect and guide the organization away from risks.

Effective Governance is dynamic, adapting as the corporate strategies and initiatives change over time. Governance must be aligned with the highest-level of strategies and objectives. It must permeate every part of the organization. Everyone must buy in.

Governance is then pushed down to the middle and lower levels of the organization. In Service Management, it can look like testing or evaluating a Change Request or evaluating how processes and practices are improved.

If the Service Value System is the architectural diagram, the Service Value Chain (SVC) is the operating model that illustrates how all the puzzle pieces fit together. It defines six key activity types onto which every value stream activity can be mapped.

The SVC becomes the way Products and Services are delivered, creating Value. ITIL4 takes value delivery in a new direction. The authors refer to this as value co-creation, with the partnership between customer and service provider. The Service Value Chain is the operating model that flows through the Service Value System, from Opportunity or Demand through Value creation.

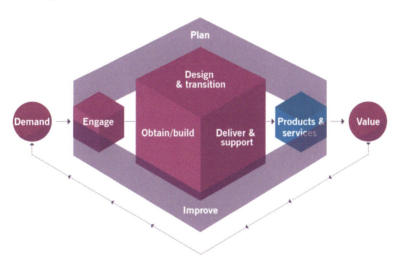

Service Management Leadership, LLC

It may be easiest to think of the SVS as the subway system of a large city and each SVC as the individual subway cars that run across the interconnected network of tracks.

The Service Value Chain includes six activities:

- Plan
- Engage
- Design & Transition
- Obtain/Build
- Deliver and Support
- Improve

Products and Services are not activities. Rather, they are what is delivered to the customer that may be viewed as "Value." We all consume services in our daily lives. It is the customer's view of "Value" that matters, but the service provider helps co-create the Value with the customer in mind.

Compared to the rigid Service Lifecycle Model of ITILV3, the Service Value Chain is flexible enough to map any route from Demand or Opportunity to Value, including all types of variables from pure in-house development to a completely sourced Product or Service from external service providers. The SVC is built to accommodate the many ways a solution is delivered to the customer. The key is the built-in flexibility.

The transition from processes to practices may change how people view ITIL4, but their role is still the same – deliver Value to customers through executing in a standardized manner.

As stated above, ITIL4 utilizes 34 of these practices. When evaluating how to proceed into ITIL4, be conscious of how the practices are interconnected. Just like with ITILV3, the output of one practice may be the input of another (e.g., Incident Management -> Problem Management).

In the previous ITIL versions, each process activity would be completed sequentially, then move onto the next process in the Service Lifecycle. But ITIL4 allows for "Value Stream Mapping." Per ITIL4, a value stream is "a series of steps an organization undertakes to create and deliver products and services to consumers," all working across the ITIL4 Service Value Chain (SVC). There is no prescribed order in ITIL4. It is the path that creates value.

Value streams happen with or without mapping. They are the natural path of moving from Demand or Opportunity through the creation of value. This can be thought of with a pair of illustrations:

39

- If there is no sidewalk, those who walk through the area will naturally walk on the grass, beating it down on the shortest path between where they originated and where they are headed. The same is for value streams. The path is natural and not prescribed.

- Another example is the flow of the river. The water will flow in the most efficient path, eroding the rocks and dirt to create a new flow. In essence, these are value streams. The river is efficient by nature, literally, and so are value streams inside technology organizations. The key is to not force value streams into a list of sequential activities.

"Improvement" or "Continual Improvement" seems to be everywhere in ITIL4. It is a practice. It is included in both the Service Value System and the Service Value Chain. The concept of continuous improvement should be included in everything we do - and how we do it. One of the easiest mechanisms to implement is a feedback loop for users and all stakeholders to provide feedback on practices, delivery, and everything else. These stakeholder groups are the people closest to Service Management execution, so they may see something that is a blind spot for Practice and Process Owners and Managers. If the goal is maturity, then it can only occur with feedback. Also, adoption will be much easier if all stakeholders feel like they are heard, and their feedback is valuable. We have all been asked for our feedback out of courtesy, and it was not taken seriously, our "care factor" and effort decreased.

40

The ITIL4 authors gave Improvement an elevated role because it is everyone's job. The final step in Improvement is finding mechanisms to measure the improvement. This is easier said than done as most metrics that measure something other than "volume" are not innately included in the ITSM toolsets. Sure, you can know how many changes or incidents occur and trend them, but how about incidents from emergency changes by group or the length of service outage and how much it cost for that bad change? Improvement metrics are the mechanism to show value to leadership and measure progress, two things every initiative requires. Continual Improvement is everyone's responsibility. There must be a culture for improvement. Think of a garden. The soil and ecological factors provide the environment for growth. The same is for improvement.

Chapter Four – Guiding Principles

Guiding Principles were in previous ITIL versions, but in ITIL4 they become a prominent aspect of the framework. These seven principles are:

1. Focus on Value.
2. Start Where You Are
3. Progress Iteratively with Feedback
4. Collaborate and Promote Visibility
5. Think and Work Holistically
6. Keep It Simple and Practical
7. Optimize and Automate

A guiding principle is a recommendation that provides universal and enduring guidance to an organization, which applies in all circumstances, regardless of its size, strategies, industry, or management structure. The 7 ITIL Guiding Principles are adapted from the 9 Guiding Principles defined in ITIL's 2016 Practitioner course. They represent the core tenets of ITIL and broader service management.

The purpose of the ITIL4 Guiding Principles is to be universally applicable to any organizational initiative, any size of organization or type of service provider, and to all relationships with stakeholder groups. Consider how this represents most of the challenges facing the technology segment of most organizations.

Organizations must have a "North Star" to help guide them when there is indecision or a lack of understanding. If someone is lost at night, they can easily look up and orient their direction based on the North Star. These Guiding Principles serve the same purpose.

Your organization may choose to identify and adopt your own Guiding Principles. That is perfectly acceptable. The goal and purpose is to help drive the organization's decisions.

These Guiding Principles are heavily influenced by Agile, LEAN, DevOps, and COBIT. In implementing ITIL4, every organization must merge it with at least one of the other frameworks. This is a tall task for most organizations. Let's take a deep look at each of the Guiding Principles as they will be key to the successful adoption of ITIL4.

1. **Focus on value** - Everything the organization does should directly or indirectly connect back to value for itself, its customers, and other stakeholders. One basic ITIL4 tenet is the concept of value co-creation, where the customer and the service provider work together to create value. The customer's feedback helps the service provider provide products and services the customer finds value in. The first step is to understand who the customers, consumers, and other stakeholders are of the service. If we know the "who," the next step is understanding what constitutes value from their perspective. If we know the "who" and "what," the last step is to measure the "how." ITIL4 takes a big step forward with the acknowledgment of customer experience (CX) and

43

user experience (UX), even incorporating them into the Service Level Agreements (SLAs) to create Experience Level Agreements (XLAs). While SLAs measure service performance, XLAs measure the user experience of using the service. Moving toward XLAs complementing SLAs will be a large step for many technology organizations.

If we ponder the role of User Experience (UX) in every aspect of our respective lives, it is only natural that it should permeate services. Leaders must consider the UX of using their services. Business stakeholders have other options.

No matter the activity, process, or practice, the focus must be on value.

2. **Start Where You Are** - When considering an ITIL4 transformation or even an improvement opportunity, you must know the starting point. It is where you are currently. Some organizations want to wipe the slate clean, but they end up throwing the baby out with the bathwater. Other organizations have an inflated view of their maturity, so they wish to start at an advanced place, making the initiative even more difficult. If we are starting where we are, it does not matter how we got here or any of the other things we hold onto too tightly. It just matters where we go from here.

Sometimes, what is currently implemented is unusable so starting from scratch is the best option, but this decision should not be made lightly. Do not start over without first

44

considering what is already available to be leveraged. Objectivity is extremely valuable. Most organizations that hit the "detonate" button and start anew do so due to comparison with other organizations or what is viewed as perfect or mature. Maturity is organization-specific and cannot be compared.

There is also a risk-management element that must be understood. Even the worst ITIL environment has aspects to utilize for improvement. For example, consider the organizational change aspects of blowing it up versus making incremental progress.

Services already in place will provide a mechanism for improvements. Acknowledge and leverage the current status as a foundation for the improvement efforts. On this note, metrics and measures should be instituted to measure progress and further become the basis for improvement.

3. **Progress Iteratively with Feedback** – The technology world has quickly moved to the various Agile frameworks. This has forced organizations to think in iterations instead of big-bang, waterfall deployments. If the year 2020 taught us nothing else, we learned that the strategic technology projects and initiatives leaders had planned for the year would soon need to change, change in strategic direction, requirements, and even what success looks like.

45

The technology cycles are speeding up, which is further making the waterfall approach obsolete. By the time an organization kicks off a one-year project, collects requirements, develops the solution, and begins testing, the project goals and objectives - along with the technology to deliver and support - have changed. In what used to take three years, organizations are delivering in six months aided by innovative technology.

This Guiding Principle is at the core of most technology departments. Work should be organized into smaller, manageable pieces that can be executed and delivered to meet time expectations. Breaking the large amount of work into smaller pieces also allows the organization to be nimble and alter course if variables change. The overall project or effort must be continually reevaluated and potentially adjusted. Feedback is important in every part of our lives. This Guiding Principle acknowledges that the iterations will adjust course based on consumer, customer, and stakeholder feedback. Seeking and incorporating feedback before, during, and after each iteration will ensure that all actions are focused on delivering value. Feedback also may be used to identify improvement opportunities.

4. **Collaborate and Promote Visibility** – Legacy IT departments fell victim to siloes. These siloes became divisive between the IT group and the customer. This Guiding Principle seeks to build bridges of collaboration between all stakeholder groups. It is a long-overdue response to the Agile and DevOps (even LEAN) environments currently gaining prominence in today's IT organizations.

If initiatives involve the appropriate people in the correct roles, all stakeholder groups begin to buy in. As we see in other areas of society, the tide rises with the inclusion of all voices and falls in exclusion (siloes). This inclusion brings different voices, more enthusiastic contributions, and even greater cross-departmental leadership support. Accomplishing as a team brings rewards both now and in the future as bridges begin to be built.

The most important step is identifying and managing all the stakeholder groups. A few prominent stakeholder groups are customers, consumers, users, suppliers, and even the security, risk, and compliance teams. There are many stakeholder groups, so the initiative must be visible to all to ensure that all relevant stakeholders are included.

Each stakeholder group has a different perspective that must be heard if the initiative hopes to be successful. Requirements, messaging, and defining what success looks like must be understood for all stakeholders.

Collaboration does not mean consensus. A decision may have to be made that some stakeholders disagree with, but the main point is that their feedback and concerns were heard. Some stakeholders may get a "voice" while others get a "vote," but that is acceptable because a decision must be made and too many with "votes" can make implementing any effort – especially ITIL4 – very difficult.

5. **Think and Work Holistically** - Building on the breaking down of siloes above, a holistic approach is needed. No service, practice, process, department, or supplier succeeds alone. If we remember back to the ITILV3 days, the outputs of one process were the inputs of another (e.g., Event Management -> Incident Management). Taking it a step further in ITIL4, the outputs an organization delivers should translate into customer outcomes. These outcomes do not occur in a bubble. They come from multiple parts working together.

If we look at the world from a holistic perspective, we see how every service comprises all four of the Four Dimensions of Service Management, plus stakeholders, and the feedback from all parties. This includes understanding how demand is captured and how it is translated into valuable outcomes. The addition, deletion, or amendment of one piece will impact another. When considering an ITIL4 transformation, a holistic viewpoint must be adapted and maintained.

The increased complexity of technology and how it is used across the enterprise forces leaders to take a holistic approach. Collaboration is needed to deliver the right outcomes.

6. **Keep It Simple and Practical** – Thinking back to the "traditional" IT groups of old, there was little that was simple or practical in the eyes of customers and stakeholders. The jargon, the systems, and everything were complex. ITIL4 is emphatically telling technology leaders that they must deliver simple and practical solutions – including terminology, practices, and everything else – even if the behind the scenes is complex. Customers only care about the part they see. They do not care about what the node is connected to (or even what a node is) or whether code is frontend or backend. They just care about understanding the service and deriving value from it. When you walk into a deli, do you care what went in to deliver a sandwich to you? Neither does a business stakeholder who only wants outcomes.

49

Keeping things simple and practical means choosing customer outcomes over the parts that make them up. This includes the metrics and measures, too. Consider what your customer thinks is important: uptime, speed-to-deliver, reduced time to resolve, fewer incidents caused by changes, etc. Sure, the Service Management group may have other metrics to measure other aspects of the service but keep things simple and practical for stakeholders.

Just like with the first Guiding Principle above, the focus should be on value. Simplicity helps the customer appreciate the value. It may mean that your group does fewer things – but at a higher level – than before. Some excellence is better than a lot of mediocrity.

Quick wins are one way to gain desired customer engagement. Every project or initiative offers opportunities to address customer requirements early on, even if on a small scale. These "quick wins" allow for speedier adoption, alignment between service consumer and service provider, and give momentum for the effort.

7. **Optimize and Automate** – These two are intrinsically joined. Optimization must occur before automation should commence. If not, you will get poor outcomes more quickly. Optimization refers to maximizing the value of work creating outcomes. Optimization may – or may not – take the form of technology, while automation is always using technology to perform tasks and activities. Optimization is always possible while Automation is not. And, it can be implemented over time.

Optimization usually refers to becoming as efficient and effective as possible. Even in a simple process like getting out of bed and going to work, optimization seeks ways to save time. LEAN is an influence on this Guiding Principle. Optimization looks for ways to make things simpler, cheaper, safer, and more consistent. It looks to make things as useful as they can be.

Automation is the use of technology to perform tasks and activities without human intervention. The key part is "without human intervention." Automation is everywhere. The event monitoring tool closing events and incidents without human involvement. The use of a chatbot for the Service Desk. The deployment of code into the environment. Each of these – and the many other examples - saves time. Automation also streamlines a task or tasks even if the whole is not automated.

51

Think about your ITSM tool. Those workflows are automation. The way the tool "knows" who needs to approve a change or how an incident is routed. This is automation. It is a large part of the technology footprint and growing because it takes the toils of tasks away from the expensive humans. There are two main benefits of automation: lowering cost because technology costs less than people (especially technology people), and allowing the teams to focus on higher value work. It also minimizes the issues arising from human error. One other aspect leaders must grasp is that technology is a capital expense (CapEx) while personnel salaries are operational expenses (OpEx). Most organizations prefer to invest in technology to reduce the annual expense of people. The roles of automation and service providers will quickly put pressure on technology leaders to reduce headcount. If we look at this in the context of adopting ITIL4, we will need to address the possibility of automating each piece through the Service Management practices.

In total, these Guiding Principles offer leaders an approach to implementing, maintaining, and maturing their Service Management program based on the ITIL4 principles.

The Guiding Principles are great starting points for all types of transformations. They can integrate or add to an organization's existing principles, service standards, or other means of organizational guidance.

Much has changed from the previous versions, and the Guiding Principles reflect today's environment with many frameworks implemented in many organizations. ITIL4 offers a path to incorporating and leveraging multiple frameworks harmoniously.

Just like everything else, success or failure is not caused by the framework but by the delivery. Value is derived from the execution.

Chapter Five – Implementation Strategy

Like many other areas in life, theory looks different than the real world. Consider how the university classroom experience in any subject differs depending on the school, the textbook used, and the professor. Algebra has changed little over the years, yet students emerge from classes with wildly different levels of mastery due to external factors. Some educators help their students understand the practical applications while it was just theory for others. For every topic, successful learning is understanding how it is applied, even if applied differently depending on the situation. Algebra is used in many ways and can be applied to many circumstances.

Similarly, ITIL changed little over the decade since ITILV3 supplanted V2, and hundreds of thousands of people took ITILV3 classes, yet the students came away with different levels of understanding how to apply what was learned. Look around many organizations and you will see the ITIL principles applied very differently. Many times, it is due to the variables at the organization, including its in-house expertise, its leadership adopting the framework, or other drivers of maturity.

Another example is law school. Millions of attorneys graduate from law school every decade, yet only the top ones understand how to apply the law's nuance reliably – or perhaps creatively -- to a unique situation. If you have a legal issue, you want to employ an attorney who understands the legal statutes, precedents, and current cases to create the best outcomes for you, the client. In the world of ITIL, this is true now more than ever. Hundreds of thousands of people will take ITIL4 classes, yet so few will know how to apply it to their specific organization.

When we look back on the many companies and government agencies adopting ITIL4 over the next few years, we will be astonished by two things:

- How successful some were compared to others (given the lack of prescription for putting ITIL4 into practice)
- The reasons for the success and the lack thereof for others

When we consider the reasons for the success, most will fall into two categories:

- Lack of expertise (either in-house or employing "experts" who cannot adopt the framework to the specific organizational needs).
- Lack of resources allocated to the effort, especially to accommodate the shifting strategies, requirements, and desired outcomes.

There will be a huge divide on levels of adoption. Like everything else, there will be some who jump in with both feet and have the backing of executive leadership. There will be other organizations whose middle and lower levels see the ITIL4 framework as an opportunity to congeal all the different advocacy groups within the organization and try to "push" the framework up through the organization chart.

When considering an "implementation" strategy, there is no universal "right way." Instead, what should be sought is the right way for the organization at the specific moment in time given all the other variables (e.g., leadership support and risk tolerance, in-house expertise, etc.). Every organization is unique. The strategy should be as well. Would you ever buy someone else's tailor-made clothes? Just as every person is created differently than others, so are corporations.

In order to identify the best strategy for your organization, see the chart below. It will offer seven broad paths for ITIL4 implementation and adoption. The chart below will illustrate some of the differentiating variables across organizations and why your specific organization needs a tailor-made strategy.

Speed	ITILV3 Maturity	Processes	In-House Expertise
Slow	High	10+	High
Medium	Medium	6+	Medium
Fast	Low	3+	Low

Let's start by looking at some basic definitions.

- Speed – The desired speed at which your organization wishes to adopt the ITIL4 framework. Some may call this "velocity." The faster the desired move to ITIL4, the greater the risk. Ask yourself what level of change your organization can handle without creating risk.
- ITILV3 Maturity – Current ITILV3 process maturity via a process and program assessment. This can be an official assessment via an outside firm or internally developed with the help of the internet.

- Processes – The number of current ITILV3 processes actively managed and owned with metrics to measure improvement. The more processes currently viable, the easier the transition to ITIL4. They provide a foundation for improvement.

- In-house Expertise – Do you objectively have the in-house expertise to transition to ITIL4? Every leader must ask themselves this one question. At the roots of the question is whether the organization can create enough change to be successful. In a vacuum, in-house expertise is one of the biggest predictors of ITIL4 adoption success. If you do not possess it currently, now is the time to train or acquire the expertise. Even having the consulting firm helping with the ITIL4 adoption provide knowledge transfer is a large step, so include it in the Statement of Work.

While this may seem complex, it will quickly turn into a basic scoring system.

- For the Speed, use a multiplier of 10 for Fast, 6 for Medium, and 2 for Slow. Speed is relative and depends on the organization, but the greater the speed to adopt the ITIL4 framework, the greater the risk to success.

- For every response on the top row (High, 10+, High), multiply by 2.
- For every answer on the middle row (Medium, 6+, Medium), multiply by 6.
- For every reply on the bottom row (Low, 3+, Low), multiply by 10.

So, in practice, one example may be:

You have an organization going through a large transformation and want to adopt the ITIL4 framework to aid in the transformation. You have an urgency to quickly transition to ITIL4 (x10). As a leader, you find an ITIL maturity assessment on the internet and determine your organization has Medium process maturity (x6) with 8 processes established (x6) and High in-house expertise (x2). Your score is 720.

Another example is:

You have an immature ITILV3 program (x10) with 3 processes (x10,) and Medium in-house expertise (x6), so you decide to slowly (x2) adopt ITIL4 because it may create too much disruption. Your score is 1,200.

One last example:

You are an executive in a stable organization with 14 (x2) mature processes (x2), and good in-house expertise (x2). Given this scenario, you decide to adopt ITIL4 at Medium speed (x6). Your score is only 48. If you decide to implement quickly, the score is only 80. Having a high number of mature processes and good in-house expertise lowers the risk. As it should.

You can probably guess that the higher the score, the greater the risk to a successful implementation/adoption. We will identify several strategies with additional strategic implications below.

The following table will help determine the appropriate strategy for your organization:

Tier	Points	Strategy
1	< 200	This is a low-risk strategy due to a slow implementation in a mature environment.
2	< 500	Still a relatively low-risk strategy. Risk will come from Speed and Maturity
3	< 750	This is on the high end of low-risk. Caution is advised as obstacles need to be addressed.

Tier	Points	Strategy
4	< 1,000	The medium-risk strategy is required to be successful given the risks.
5	< 1,250	As we move into the dangerous scenarios, risk is increasing. So is the need to identify the appropriate strategy.
6	< 1,500	A very risky scenario requiring a specific strategy to be successful. The greater the risk, the greater the need for a specific strategy to address the risk.
7	> 1,500	The highest-risk strategy needing extra guidance and resources.

When running through the myriad of scenarios, the one common driver for strategies is the Speed and leadership's urgency to transition to ITIL4. Multiplying your other variables by 10 drives up risk ... as it should if the implementation must occur quickly to align with transformation or other initiatives.

Before we get into the unique strategies, let's discuss risk. Risk comes in many varieties and flavors. There is risk in doing something and risk in doing nothing. Anytime we implement something new, we create risk. Risk is increased if there is a lack of stability in the environment or if the organization cannot handle the rate of change. This is why the speed-to-implement multiplier is important.

61

Regardless of which strategy you fall into, there are three variables they each have in common:

1. A defined strategy is required for adopting the ITIL4 framework, including speed and impact to other initiatives.
2. An ITIL program and process assessment to objectively evaluate the current state.
3. An objective view of the in-house talent and expertise. They will be the main people on the front lines of the initiative, and junior resources may not be able to support a speedy transition to ITIL4. People create outcomes. The better the people, the better the outcomes.

There are a few unmeasurable factors to consider before we get into the specific strategies. One is leadership stability and resolve to deliver the desired outcomes. This is a big element as we all know that we cannot measure leadership's motives, priorities, or ability. A couple of other bits of guidance:

- When transitioning to ITIL4, prioritize maturity over adding new processes or practices. Very few organizations implemented all 26 ITILV3 processes, and even fewer will implement all 34 of the ITIL4 practices. So, do not succumb to the temptation that more is better. Maturity trumps quantity because it enables a faster rate of change.

- ITILV3 was tremendously prescriptive in that it gave detailed steps to progress through a list of process activities for each process as you moved through the Service Lifecycle. ITIL4 is not prescriptive in either the practice activity steps or how to go through the Service Value Chain.

There will be multiple paths to adopting ITIL4, but they each start with the ITIL4 Guiding Principle of "Start Where You Are." This is why having the objective program and process assessment is important. So is an objective view of the in-house personnel. We all know people who see themselves differently in the mirror than what is reality. For example, I know a teenage young man with a few hairs on the top of his upper lip, under his nose. When he looks in the mirror, he sees a 1970s-style, Tom Selleck mustache. Others see it much differently. The same is true for Service Management organizations. Some leaders see their organizations as more mature than they are in reality. But just like with the young man, objectivity is key.

The second step for all strategies is another Guiding Principle, "Progress Iteratively With Feedback." This is a common starting point for every organization. The rate of iteration will turn into the speed-to-transition to ITIL4. For clarity, we advocate an iterative approach, not big-bang, as the variables and needs of the business will change over time, and a nimble approach is required.

63

The first Guiding Principle discussed earlier, "Focus on Value." is also important to remember. As every technology strategy should be aligned with a broader corporate strategy, every transformation should be focused on delivering value to stakeholders. This is especially true when deciding which path to undertake for transitioning to ITIL4.

Now, let's look at strategies for each of the scores above, starting with the least-risky tier.

1. If your organization scores in Tier 1, you have a stable environment for change. You have mature processes and solid in-house expertise. Organizations do not score in this tier by accident. There is usually less organizational change overall – compared to the higher tiers – and so the speed can be High and the initiative still low-risk. If you are in this tier, the strategies should contain three aspects:

   a. Impact analysis on the existing stable environment.

   b. Roles and responsibilities for in-house staff so they do not take on more responsibility than they can handle. They are an asset. Treat them like one.

c. Transitioning one ITILV3 process to an ITIL4 practice at a time will minimize impact and risk. The order of process-to-practice adoption should be based on least-disruptive to greatest. Plus, some practices should be established before adopting the Service Value System.

2. If your organization is in Tier 2, you are still risk-averse and possess a stable environment. This is an advantage to leverage. Your strategy will look similar to the one above but have some subtle differences. Here are three differences from Tier 1:

a. Since you can still support a High rate of speed, you need to be able to measure the results to measure progress. Metrics and Key Performance Indicators (KPIs) should be established.

b. Given the strong in-house expertise, Process Owners and Managers should have plans to engage business stakeholders.

c. Informal or formal training will need to be developed to ensure that all stakeholders, users, and Process Managers are on the same page in terms of strategies, expectations, and creating a common vision of what success looks like.

3. If your organization falls in Tier 3, there is good news: you can adapt much of the above two tiers and add two basic elements. Tier 3 is where initiatives begin entering the risky territory. One could see this as when you go to the doctor and she says your blood pressure is in the "good" category, but not far from the average levels, so keep a close eye on things. The same guidance applies here. Tier 3 should include:

a. To minimize risk, the Configuration Management Database (CMDB) and its inherent discovery capabilities must be well-established. Accurate reporting is a must. A stable CMDB will lessen the risk level since it is the foundation for every ITILV3 process and ITIL4 Service Management practice.

b. Published and visible balanced metrics will lessen the risk as they will serve as both milestone enlightenment and a compass if the ITIL4 adoption veers off course. Given that "Measurement and Reporting" is a formal ITIL4 practice, having solid reporting capabilities is needed for a successful ITIL4 implementation, whether as a practice or as a one-off capability. This reporting may come from the ITSM toolset, business intelligence tools, or a combination of both. The key is to publish the metrics, measures, and all KPIs and trending those over time.

4. If your organization falls in Tier 4, take heart. You have only moderate risk and can handle any of the options for speed-to-implement. To reach the 750-999 points, your organization has some key building blocks to leverage for the move to ITIL4. These should be the areas you lean on for the initiative. Two more elements should be added to the previous guidance:

a. Organizational Change Management (OCM), now an official ITIL4 practice, should be utilized to lessen the risk. The degree to which OCM is implemented should depend on the desired speed to adopt ITIL4. The greater the speed, the greater the need for OCM. OCM has a direct impact on stakeholder adoption and should not be taken for granted.

b. With increased risk, there is also an increased need to regularly engage stakeholders, including metrics review. Further, this engagement should be used to align the ITIL4 initiative strategy with that of the business customer and the organization as a whole. This alignment lessens risk as it allows the initiative to pivot to a new strategy and plan if needed. The lack of stakeholder engagement is a billboard for inducing risk.

67

Service Management Leadership, LLC

5. As we enter the first high-risk tier, Tier 5, your strategies will start to look different from the low-risk ones. Yes, the guidance for those still applies, but the focus moves to lowering the risk levels so that the transition to ITIL4 will be successful. Two changes are needed from the previous strategies. First, Communication Plans must be established for both the ITIL4 transformation and for the individual practices. Consider the need for optimal communication in Incident Management (including Major Incident Management), Change Enablement, and Service Level Management, just to name a few. The success of the practices, including what has changed, is a requirement for success. Second, in Tier 4, we discussed the need for OCM. It is still a requirement, but the level of Organizational Change Management has increased with the risk level. As we move into the higher-risk tiers, organizational change must be handled through the use of personas. An OCM Plan will include how to address, communicate, and plan for change with different groups of stakeholders or personas. Personas are merely groups of people with some commonality. As risk increases, so does the need to collaborate with ALL stakeholders.

6. Organizations do not reach Tier 6 without having two things in common: a need for speed-to-adopt ITIL4 and a low ITILV3 process maturity. This is quite the explosive mix. To minimize the risk, there are two things to consider. First, as stated before, there should be an effort to mature existing ITILV3 processes before transitioning to ITIL4 practices. But some organizations may desire to make the leap to ITIL4 BECAUSE the ITILV3 processes are immature. This is OK, but risk is present. Consider how your organization can put guardrails on the transition to reduce risk. One such way may be to add resources, internal or external. Using metrics, it becomes easier to measure the progress of external partners. Second, since Speed is an important variable for your organization, the balance between risk and Speed is important. There may be times the iterations slow momentarily to address risk. This may include risk from resource unavailability, other transformation activities, or even tool implementation.

7. If your organization is at Tier 7, your risk tolerance is high, and the pressure to deliver results matches it. This is totally fine as long as goals are reasonable, and you can procure the needed resources to be successful. Your strategy should include one main piece not described above. Since success is measured on the transition to ITIL4, you MUST be willing to live with immature aspects for a while. You will rely heavily on the Guiding Principle of "Iterating" to slowly get better and more mature. It is advised that you continue to objectively measure program and practice maturity and in-house expertise as risk has been added.

There are a few leading tenets for every organization transitioning to ITIL4:

- The greater the risk, the greater the need to establish a mechanism for capturing Demand and Opportunities. This is for both strategic and operational reasons. How will you be successful if you cannot understand how your business customers give you work?
- Once again, focus on what your stakeholders will consider as adding value.
- With increased risk, communication becomes more important. Communication comes in many forms, and all are needed in the high-risk tiers.

- On the topic of OCM, success may depend on organizational buy-in to understand value, not just doing it because everyone is now forced into adopting. Forced adoption is not adoption. Those of us with teenagers know this is true. Someone will do things because they must, but they will not do so to their highest ability. Plus, if there is no buy-in, personnel will not be actively seeking improvement opportunities.

- Quick wins should be identified at the outset of the initiative. Quick wins lead to understanding what is important and showing value in that regard. In addition, success should be socialized and celebrated. If success is hidden, is it really a success?

- Your initiative will not be successful if just pushed down from the top or if the bottom layers of the organization attempt to push the effort up the organizational chart. Success depends on every layer of the company working together as a team.

As discussed above, the aspect of "Speed" is one of the greatest influences of risk, and risk has a big influence on your chance of success. When considering strategies, try to understand how risk may be reduced. There are mechanisms – like leveraging external partners (e.g., Service Management Leadership) to lower risk while increasing speed.

71

Many agilists will use the term "velocity," and it applies to this situation, too, as organizations will seek to gain velocity in their transition to ITIL4.

With technology spreading throughout the enterprise like a wildfire, ITIL4 can help your organization break down siloes and help the enterprise see Service Management as a mechanism to manage ALL technology with a business view. This is what executives will demand for the next decade as traditional IT and "the business" slowly morph into one.

Chapter Six – Potential Obstacles to Success

While pondering the best ITIL4 strategy for your organization, there are some other considerations, specifically potential obstacles impeding your success. These challenges come in many varieties and may not all apply to your organization. As stated many times, every company or government agency is unique, so the strategies and obstacles will mirror the uniqueness.

Let's start with the obstacles which will affect most organizations:

1. ITSM Tools – The ITSM toolmakers are still using ITILV3 nomenclature and workflows. For example, Change Management is used instead of Change Enablement in the tools currently on the market. In addition, the workflows still follow the Service Lifecycle. If you are wondering why this might impede your success, consider that your organization will be using multiple names for the same thing. Confusion will arise. Any type of distraction is an obstacle, especially one so foundational like the tool

73

2. Following up on the above, metrics inside the ITSM tools will be using the ITILV3 terminology. While this may not seem like a huge challenge, consider how organizations wishing to leverage the new ITIL4 capabilities may be measuring the wrong things if still using ITILV3 naming, metrics, workflows, and the Service Lifecycle aspects. Companies who integrate dashboards into their ITSM tool will also be impacted for the same reasons.

3. As mentioned before, clearing up the confusion of "Change Management" will not be easy as so many areas of a company or government agency use this term to reflect the authorization and movement of changes into production. But in ITIL4, it now means Organizational Change Management. In an attempt to not confuse stakeholders, Organizational Change Management will be needed for the name change, ironically enough. Further, non-ITIL standards like ISO and CoBit still use "Change Management" in the same way as ITILV3. This could cause confusion with auditors and other external stakeholders. ITIL is on an island regarding this term. It is neither right nor wrong, but needs to be understood by all parties.

4. Many – if not most – organizations were designed off the ITILV3 Service Lifecycle model. While that may or may not surprise most readers, consider how Service Operations has been isolated – and even outsourced to external service providers – in many organizations. The outsourcing may be for all or part of Service Operations. But when we consider ITIL4 in this context, integrating multiple external and internal Operations service providers with the multiple Development service providers may prove a sizable challenge. ITIL4 is set up to handle DevOps and this includes the Development and Operations of the service. This specific obstacle will grow over time unless the Service Management organization can mature and adapt to the stakeholders' needs while showing value.

5. As noted several times, ITIL4 is less prescriptive than ITILV3. You may be wondering what this means and why it is relevant. The ITILV3 books detailed each process inside the five Service Lifecycle books. This information included CSFs, KPIs, Interactions with other Processes, and most importantly, Process Activities. The Process Activities were a step-by-step guide. These Process Activities were so detailed and strong that the ITSM tools copied them for their respective workflows. But the ITIL4 books are more theory than practice, leaving organizations wondering how to adapt what is best for them instead of having a follow-the-steps guide. This is one of the main reasons we wanted to write this book and start Service Management Leadership. The ambiguity is too much for many organizations already in the midst of other transformations.

6. If your organization is moving to ITIL4, you will need to update your process (practice) documentation to reflect the changes. Wholesale documentation upgrades are not easy and require stakeholder engagement as the stakeholders' needs have changed since the process/practice was last documented. This may include the policy document, the process documentation, and the procedures. This documentation overhaul is not easy to do while trying to move to ITIL4 and while still performing "normal" job functions. This is one area an external service provider (like Service Management Leadership) can help.

7. If your organization has addressed all of the above, consider the need to update all metrics to reflect what is important in ITIL4. The metrics may shift focus from technology to the customers and their experience and satisfaction with your services. These metrics will need considerable thought to measure only what is important and to forego all that is not.

77

8. We have mentioned many external obstacles, but one of the largest internal obstacles may be the quality of the CMDB for many organizations. This is the foundation of your Service Management program and needs to be mature, offering current and accurate data on every service component. The CMDB is a tool-specific area for many organizations while maturity comes from the process/practice side. Improvement in CMDB health will help other practices. One note: ITIL4 splits the ITILV3 Service Asset and Configuration Management process into Configuration Management (CMDB) and IT Asset Management (including both Hardware and Software Asset Management). The separation permits further focus on the CMDB to support the other Service Management practices.

With all the obstacles, some organizations may choose to "adopt and adapt" very little while others will be "all in." This is ok as it will become "Utility" for every organization. Remember that term? It means "Fit for Purpose." These strategies and obstacles are organization-specific.

Those that adopt slowly should consider cherry-picking ITIL4 for ways to improve. Why not just adopt the pieces that offer the most bang for your effort, those that offer the most value for stakeholders? Those looking to transition to ITIL4 to a larger degree should also prioritize the roadmap to first focus only on the areas that offer the best Return on Investment (ROI) or value before transitioning to the lower-value targets. Every organization must decide how and when to put ITIL4 into practice.

Chapter Seven – Execution Plan

Executing the strategies listed above will not be easy. Run away from those who say it will be, or from those who think their one-size-fits-most strategy will work for you and your unique organizational variables. So, how should we start?

Here is a checklist to monitor success:

Step	Action Needed
1	ITIL4 Foundations
2	Assessment
3	Roadmap
4	Show Value
5	Align Internally
6	Align Externally
7	Integrate Tools and Metrics
8	Integrate Materials
9	Improvement Opportunities
10	Stakeholder Engagement
11	Governance
12	Speed
13	Knowledge Management
14	Slow, But Iterative Approach

1. Send stakeholders through ITIL4 Foundations. As you embark down this path, a common language (terminology) is key. If transitioning to ITIL4, with so many challenges and obstacles, you will need many educated on foundation-level basics from all stakeholder groups. As mentioned in Chapter 6, having different definitions for "Change Management" will inhibit success unless everyone is singing the same tune ... so to speak. If you - as a leader - have teams of people who have gone through ITIL4 Foundations and are anxious to migrate toward ITIL4, you have options. You can transition to the framework quickly or slowly. However, the worst thing you can do is remain status quo. It is bad for morale to show people the new capabilities but choose not to take advantage of them. If you send people through foundations, show them how their new training fits inside the larger ITIL4 transformation plan. Everyone just wants to know their respective role.

2. Next, we have mentioned several times the need for a process and practice assessment. This can be via an outside consulting firm or in-house. It does not need to be complex. Instead, an objective, accurate "GPS" location of the current status is required. Do you know people who – when they look in the mirror – see themselves as better looking, more muscular, less attractive, or even heavier than they are in real life? This is true for organizations, too. Many see their organization as more (or less) mature than it really is, with their people better (or worse) equipped to accomplish their goals, or better (or worse) able to handle the planned rate of change. This lack of objective view will only complicate the transition to ITIL4. Start Where You Are – Now is the time to act. The process assessment should be enlightening. Just as many see themselves differently than actuality, the same is true for Service Management maturity. You need to start from this GPS location. When you visit an amusement park, shopping mall, or other large venue, you will notice a large map on display with a star and the words "you are here" indicating your current location. It is the same for your Service Management program and ITIL process maturity. As you contemplate the first of many steps – and plot on a roadmap – your thoughts should be how to permit flexibility while still providing value to all stakeholders.

3. The roadmap must have the ability to pivot as you take an iterative execution approach. The roadmap must be driven by the stakeholders' view of "value." The iterations will offer feedback, and you will soon understand how much change your organization can withstand.

4. Considering the rate at which technology is expanding into non-traditional IT areas, the Service Management organization must be able to show value early and often. Understanding this in the context of transitioning to ITIL4 is a huge step. Add the non-IT technology assets to the scope of your Service Management organization as soon as possible to ensure one common set of processes and practices for the entire enterprise.

5. As stated a few times earlier, it will be people who determine your success. Set expectations. Train your staff. Educate your business stakeholders and users. Align what the people are doing with the greater organizational strategy. Many leaders make this more complex than it needs to be.

6. Make sure that your external service providers and partners are adopting ITIL4, too. If you have outsourced Operations to three different companies, and each is using the ITIL frameworks differently, you may have a problem. Additionally, the process and program maturity of each party will impact your overall initiative.

7. As mentioned in Chapter 6, the ITSM tools are still using the ITILV3 terminology, metrics, and workflows. They do not have a plan to change. Have a strategy to integrate that with your ITIL4 practices and metrics.

8. Since the ITILv3 books went into great detail about each process (and process activities plus metrics), and the ITIL4 practices do not go into much detail, you may still need to use the ITILV3 books. But doing so may create confusion, so plan accordingly. Your roadmap must include metrics, practice activities, service value mappings, etc. When implementing ITIL4, the ITILv3 material is still needed. The good news is that most mature Service Management programs will be able to leverage the existing processes as they move toward practices. These organizations will use their strong ITILV3 base to propel the initiative forward while having a strong base.

9. With the perpetual need to improve and mature processes/practices, include a mechanism for practice improvement. This improvement appears in every facet of ITIL4. It allows a way to iteratively mature and is the reason "Start Where You Are" is important for all organizations. If not already present, a mechanism for capturing, vetting, and putting into practice improvement opportunities must be established. Improvement may be getting better at what you are currently doing or doing something new (adding scope to the current state).

10. Organization siloes must be addressed. This needs to be addressed in both strategy development and execution. The question for all leaders should become, "How can we include all stakeholders in the initiative?" The follow-up questions should revolve around building relationships, developing and measuring engagement, and understanding the Opportunities and Demands.

11. Another subject that must be addressed is Governance. Yes, we discussed it earlier, but Governance – for the initiative, the Service Management organization, and the expanding role of technology must be addressed. Governance will look differently depending on the organization. Some will want centralized Governance while others decentralized. The purpose and goal of Governance are different from what most think. Governance is just a mechanism for leadership to understand the environment (including changes and their respective impacts) and make decisions appropriately.

12. Speed and velocity are under your control, so as you develop your roadmap, make sure the pace of transitioning to ITIL4 is reflected. As stated above, this is the only variable you can directly control from the outset. Use this power wisely.

13. One asset to leverage to improve your chance of unmitigated success is strong Knowledge Management. This will include the Knowledge Bases, Run Books, a way to give all stakeholders a full understanding of the current environment before the initiative begins, and an understanding of how things change as the ITIL4 transition transpires. Many see Knowledge Management as just a tool for the Service Desk. This is a great use. But Knowledge Management can impact every bit of your Service Management organization by providing a foundation of understanding both at the onset and during an initiative. Do not underestimate the impact of Knowledge Management on decision-making.

14. Given the large number of ITILV3 processes (26), those organizations with mature Service Management organizations and many established processes did not get to that level immediately. Resist the temptation to transition all or many at once. Comparison to other organizations will only cause heartache. Use an iterative process, and your speed-to-implement can be at the right pace for your organization. Your organization is unique with many unique variables. Tailor-make your roadmap for your specific organization.

This is a lot of information to digest. The strategies and execution are complex. Taking an iterative approach and including all stakeholders will ensure that – even if you miscalculate one or more variables – you can adjust and still be successful.

One consideration to ponder: attempt to identify low-hanging fruit so the progress and improvement can be shown, and adoption increased.

Chapter Eight – Critical Success Factors

In every part of our lives, we have Critical Success Factors (CSFs). A CSF is a leadership term for an element that is necessary for an organization or project to achieve its mission. As the name might suggest, CSFs are things that must happen for the initiative to be successful. When considering whether an ITIL4 initiative is successful, there are a few CSFs relevant to every organization and a few more that are organization-specific. If we think of ITIL4 from a business standpoint, what got us this far (in terms of processes and metrics) will not get us to where we want to be. ITIL4 enables new and different capabilities. We then must find a way to measure the new capabilities and outcomes.

Here are a few broad CSFs to consider. There are many more we could include, but these are the ones that are consistent across most organizations.

- Is there organizational and leadership support?
- Does leadership understand the value gained by adopting ITIL4?
- Are goals in place for the initiative?
- Are the goals measurable?
- What other measures are in place?

- Are viable metrics and measures in place to measure improvement?
- Are adequate resources (personnel, monetary, and technology) available throughout the life of the ITIL4 initiative?
- Is there a good balance of people, process, and tools?
- Is the culture receptive to the change?
- Is there enough in-house expertise to be successful long-term?
- Are you able to identify and assess the current state as a starting point and measure growth against it?
- Is there a "front door" to IT services (e.g., Service Desk, ITSM tool, etc.)?
- With the focus on iterative improvement, is there a culture for improvement?
- Is scope defined (e.g., practices, CMBD configuration items, and future scope placed on a roadmap)?
- Are all stakeholders identified and engaged?
- Is there a mechanism for stakeholders to provide feedback? Is it accepted and considered?
- Is Customer Experience and Satisfaction measured or will it be in the near future?
- Will training be developed for all stakeholders?
- Does the Service Management organization have the appropriate level of Governance?

- Do all service providers – internal and external – use the same processes and practices?
- Is the organization able to pivot and alter course as business objectives change?

That was quite the list of CSFs. Most organizations should only adopt a few at a time to improve their chances of success. There are some interesting, organization-specific CSFs. Here are a few:

- Is there a mechanism to regularly capture customer Demand and Opportunities?
- Is there regular engagement with the business stakeholders to ensure alignment?
- Is speed-to-delivery improving?
- Is service uptime improving?
- Are all assets identified and in the Asset Register and CIs in the CMDB?
- Is the organization able to handle the rate of change?
- Are the Process/Practice Owners willing to be accountable for their respective areas?
- "Governance" and "Improvement" are key areas of ITIL4. Is the organization investing in these two areas?

91

The Critical Success Factors will depend on the organization as every company or government agency will define success differently.

Once CSFs are established – and they can evolve over time – Key Performance Indicators (KPIs) should be established. No, we are not talking about the process or practice level. Rather, the initiative to adopt and adapt ITIL4 in your organization. These are high-level KPIs, aligned with CSFs and the organizational strategy. The question should always be, "Are we measuring the right things?". There should be a mechanism to measure success. Sadly, many organizations have KPIs without CSFs, which leads to measuring the wrong things, or performing measurements misaligned with the bigger picture.

Most organizations track the project time and budget, but we want to go further. The initiative to adopt and adapt ITIL4 should have measurable results. Some of them include:

- Improved speed-to-deliver
- Improved Customer Experience and Satisfaction
- Stakeholder engagement is improving
- Improving service provider performance
- Lower cost of services
- Decrease the risk to the organization
- Improve customer uptime
- All stakeholders understand the value of ITIL4

As stated above, the metrics and measures for the processes will change as you move to practices because the focus will change from the Service Lifecycle to the Service Value Chain. With the lack of ITIL4 adoption by the ITSM toolsets, this could lead organizations to continue using the ITILV3 metrics inside the toolsets, keeping separate metrics for the new ITIL4 aspects. Be warned: this may become a massive headache.

As business and organization needs change, so should the CSFs, KPIs, and all metrics. These must be aligned. As mentioned a little earlier, alignment comes from the top. CSFs should be aligned with organizational strategy. What is important at the highest levels? Those should be addressed in the CSFs. Then, align and tie those to the KPIs to ensure the right things are measured. If the organization is adopting ITIL4, it must be to satisfy or align with the organizations top-level goals.

Thankfully, the ITIL4 authors created the Measurement and Reporting practice (see above) to offer guidance. The authors discuss how the purpose of this practice is to "support good decision-making and continual improvement by decreasing the levels of uncertainty." If we think about this statement in the context of CSFs and KPIs, we must make sure to only measure the things that aid decision-making and identify improvement opportunities.

93

The ITIL4 practice also includes the three reasons for measuring:

- Performance
- Maturity
- Compliance

One other consideration when discussing measurements and metrics is the utilization of both leading and lagging indicators. Leading indicators tell us what is about to happen while lagging indicators tell us what has already happened. For leaders, leading indicators are very important as they aid decision-making.

Most of us are familiar with one type of leading indicator: the percentage chance of rain for the day. It shapes our behaviors and decision-making. You will decide what to wear and whether to bring an umbrella based on this leading indicator.

In the technology services realm, there are plenty of leading indicators, if we just take the time to look. Looking at the incoming requests for new functionality (Opportunities), we should see trends and adjust resources accordingly. Technology leaders can use this information and go meet with their business stakeholders to better understand these opportunities – and get in front of the issue instead of being reactive.

Over the years, we have seen so many metrics we call "watermelon" metrics. They look "green" and in good shape from the outside, but the further you press (or cut) in, the more you see "red." Having solid CSFs and KPIs, and monitoring them over time, will help you have the right metrics for your organization at the right time. One of the best examples of a "watermelon" metric was found in the software asset management console of an ITSM tool. The metric showed "green," which meant the organization was correctly licensed for that specific software title. However, when clicked on to dive deeper, the "green" metric looked "red" as the organization was licensed for 13 entitlements and was using 0. There was a glaring improvement opportunity.

Another example was the Director over Incident and Problem Management, who would manually "adjust" the priority of incidents and problems to make his area look better. His boss knew about it (and endorsed the behavior), and the business stakeholders soon figured it out, causing a lack of trust. These metrics looked great on the surface, but once a business stakeholder "cut" into them, it was obvious that the metrics were "red."

95

Watermelon metrics can show up anywhere, but cannot come from volume metrics. Volume metrics do not have depth; they just report the number of things. Finding out some of your metrics are watermelon - and not green through-and-through – can be a positive as they offer the long-term benefit of improvement. Finding "red" can be an improvement opportunity you would not have found anyway.

For metrics and measures (including CSFs and KPIs) to effectively drive decisions, behaviors, and identifying improvement opportunities, they have to be visible throughout the organization. Sadly, many organizations make it difficult for all stakeholders to understand the status of performance, maturity, and compliance. These metrics and measures should not only be widely publicized, but they should also be used in discussions with stakeholders, moving the conversations from subjective, opinion-based to objective, data-based.

Whether you are measuring external service providers, or the compliance of internal services, consistency and objectivity are key to gaining buy-in from all stakeholders. One common quote bears this out, "data does not lie, just the people who use it." Your stakeholders must have faith that the metrics and measures are objectively accurate.

Think of this as a scale. Many people have a bathroom scale and weigh themselves regularly. These people make diet and exercise decisions (not to mention clothes-buying decisions) off the scale metrics, expecting the output to be objective and accurate. Business stakeholders are similar in their expectations for metrics.

The concept of measuring multiple external service providers is a very real requirement for many organizations. ITIL4 challenges the traditional volume metrics and asks leaders to measure the service from the business stakeholders' point of view. One example may be quantifying the cost of an external service provider outage. In the past, IT leaders asked for credits from the external service provider, but – in reality – the cost is far more than just the credit for downtime as a percentage of the month, quarter, or year. We are now encouraged to consider the business impact of the downtime. This may include lost sales, increased chance for customer churn, negative media attention, and opportunity costs of internal personnel who could be working on something other than restoring service.

97

One of the main drivers for writing this book was to challenge leaders to focus – and measure – what is important, not just what we have always done. Our business customers are asking for (or demanding) new capabilities. This should change how we accept their requests all the way through how the services are delivered. We cannot deliver large amounts of new Opportunities using old methods.

On the topic of metrics and measurements, all that is important is measuring the right things. Your IT strategy should be aligned with the overall corporate strategy. Metrics need to measure this alignment. The remaining metrics must illustrate the execution of the strategy. If they are measuring something else, it is a wasted opportunity.

Chapter Nine – Concluding Remarks

Transitioning from ITILV3 to ITIL4 may not be the decision for some organizations, at least right away. In contrast, others will want to leverage some of the new intrinsic capabilities within the new framework to enable speed-to-delivery, iterative work cycles, and sourcing partners for the Service Value Chain, among other new capabilities. The decisions of "if," "when," and "how" to adopt the ITIL4 framework will be organization-specific.

Judging the success of adopting ITIL4 may take longer than expected because the metrics are not "volume" metrics. Success will not depend on the volume of changes handled or incident resolution times. Those will be assumed. The next generation of metrics will be focused on the customer experience, lowering risk, and minimizing siloes.

As you contemplate transitioning to ITIL4, consider that velocity (or speed) is the only variable you have direct control of at the outset. The other variables depend on what is currently in place, so it will take time to change. When going on a road trip, for example, how soon and safely you get to your destination will be based on your speed.

How soon and safe you get to your destination will be based on your speed. The greater the speed the greater the risk. Think of the long-term impacts of ITIL4 maturity. It will take time to improve. So, will the number of processes/practices. This is also true for in-house expertise. They all reflect current conditions and require time and resources to improve. Speed is the only thing you can directly control in the short-term.

If you have a "need for speed" - like the famous quote in "Top Gun," focus on Governance and Improvement. Each will enable speed of adoption.

Moving to ITIL4 is a huge step for many technology organizations as the pressures to become more efficient and effective are increasing. So are cost pressures. With technology spreading outside of the traditional IT organizations, there is an opportunity for what was once known as "IT Service Management (ITSM)" to become "Enterprise Service Management," not because the ITSM tool workflows are applied to other business areas, e.g., Human Resources. Rather, it will be because the Service Management organization has shown enough value governing the traditional IT services that senior leaders will want the same standardized approach for all technology within an organization. This will be a big step as so many new technologies are introduced every year, yet the ITIL4 framework can adapt to each.

100

Automation and leveraging technology for Service Management will become prominent in the next decade. Companies and government agencies will seek to move past manual processes.

This will have a two-pronged effect:

1. Competitive advantage.
2. Increased flexibility.

The speed and improved quality of services that the technology-leveraged automation enables will improve the quality of services for all service providers.

ITIL4 supports this seismic shift and offers needed governance, greater speed, improved accuracy, and optimized costs to the business stakeholders.

Hopefully, this book has given you things to ponder for your organization as the move to ITIL4 will not be easy, but it would yield valuable results if the strategies offered are followed.

101

Two closing remarks every reader must understand:

- Metrics and measures will be needed to measure progress, even if metrics are a blend of ITILV3 and ITIL4. How will you communicate – or even recognize – success if you do not objectively measure the progress and understand the goal? Further, all stakeholders must believe in the objectivity and accuracy of the metrics.
- Given that there is no one-size-fits-all (or even most) strategy or solution, there is no right answer for your organization so do not compare your organization to another. The old quote, "Comparison is the thief of joy" is applicable as you will never be happy with your initiative while comparing your progress to that of another organization. There are so many variables in play (e.g., ITILV3 process maturity, culture, leadership risk-tolerance, strategy and direction, and use of external service providers, among others) that influence goals, timing, and what success might look like. Even the slightest difference, like the choice or number of external service providers, may make a large difference in the ease to transition of ITIL4.

102

You may – or may not – be equipped in-house to adopt the ITIL4 framework. It is ok either way. The most important thing is to understand your GPS "you are here" spot and not view the situation more positively or negatively than is actual.

All of the variables unique to each organization will differentiate how ITIL4 will look in each company or government agency. This is what is supposed to happen. Each ITIL version is just a framework to be applied to the situation. Every organization is unique, and within a given organization, ITIL4 will mirror its uniqueness, accounting for its risk tolerance, leadership quality, and company culture.

When attorneys come out of law school, the burden is on the students to apply the law correctly for the situation. The same is true for ITIL, especially ITIL4. As noted above, ITIL4 is less prescriptive than previous versions, so organizations are offered more flexibility. Flexibility may be positive (if seen as adaptable) or negative (if seen as lacking direction).

Having a trusted external partner to help you plan your roadmap, educate stakeholders, establish an OCM Plan, and set up metrics may be needed so budget accordingly. Your transition to ITIL4 may take a couple of years, so spending a few dollars at the beginning will pay off immensely over time. It is better to take a slow, iterative approach than attempt too much at the onset.

We have stated several times that technology is sprawling outside of the traditional IT department. It should be seen as an opportunity. Now is the time for executive leadership to see the IT group execute at a high level. If this is to occur, Service Management will be the guardrails for all the technology throughout the enterprise. It will use Service Management principles, practices, processes, people, and tools for non-IT technology. The time is coming quickly. Now is the time to get your Service Management house in order and show value to the entire executive team. Service Management permits an organization to take a business-centric view of its technology, no matter where the technology resides.

Service Management Leadership, LLC was established to offer direction and help organizations with solutions for challenges like adopting ITIL4.

Acknowledgements

I want to thank the following people for their help in getting this book published.

David Billouz, Kenny Hosey, Jeevan Lobo, Waseem Ahmed, and Steven Ollek for reviewing the book and providing feedback. Their respective and collective feedback was invaluable.

I also want to thank Balaji Venkataswamy at Sky10 for the book cover design and his continued marketing strategy and execution.

Many people have provided great sounding boards for me over the years. In fear of leaving some out, we will not name names. Thank you to all who have supported Service Management Leadership, the podcasts, the books, the YouTube channel, and the company.

www.ingramcontent.com/pod-product-compliance
Lightning Source LLC
LaVergne TN
LVHW072050060326
832903LV00054B/384